Glory, Oh My

MW01703170

10 ART SONG ARRANGEMENTS OF NEGRO SPIRITUALS

Colin Lett

MICOUSTIC Media, LLC
micousticmedia.com

MM-022

For Medium Voice

ISBN: 978-1-961770-02-7

About the Composer

Colin Lett, Composer/Conductor

A native of Selma, AL, Colin Lett holds a Master of Divinity from the Samuel DeWitt Proctor School of Theology at Virginia Union University, a Master of Arts in Choral Conducting, and a Bachelor of Arts in Vocal Music from Morgan State University. Colin has four musical arrangements in circulation in the African American Church Music Series of GIA Publications, Inc. and two musical arrangements in the Jason Max Ferdinand Choral Series of Walton Publications. Colin is the conductor of the Suitland High School Center for the Visual and Performing Arts Choir and an ordained Baptist minister. He is a life member of Alpha Phi Alpha Fraternity, Inc., Phi Mu Alpha Sinfonia Fraternity of America, Inc., and a Friend of the Arts of Sigma Alpha Iota International Music Fraternity, Inc.

Glory, Oh My Soul!

10 Art Song Arrangements of Negro Spirituals

PREFACE

"Glory! Glory! Glory, oh my soul!
Glory! Glory! Don't you wanna go...?"

This collection of art song arrangements was written over a 20-year span, from my days as a vocal music major at Morgan State University, through my seminary days at Virginia Union University, and into my days as a music educator in Alabama and Maryland. Centered around the theme of heaven, this collection calls for a wide array of emotional expressions and inspirations: some joy, some sorrow, some longing, some peace, some pleading, and some praise. Interpretively, singers are allowed great artistic license and are encouraged to be the final step of the creative process. I hope experiencing this music will, for a moment in time, help musicians and audiences alike transcend the troubles of the world and commune with God through the heavenly bliss of our ancestors' sacred songs.

Special thanks to friends who commissioned and performed several of these arrangements over the years. Thanks to my Lett, Cleggs, and Micou families for my Christian and musical roots. Thank you to the wonderful music educators who poured so much into me at Morgan State University and Selma High School (Selma, AL). Finally, I thank God for the memory of my mother, Mrs. Rita Micou Lett, to whom this collection is lovingly dedicated.

Colin Lett

MM-022

Glory, Oh My Soul!

for Medium Voice

Colin Lett

arr. "Oh Glory" and "I Got a New Name"

14
death shall be no more?
Glor-y! Glor-y!
Glor-y, oh my
Pno.
B
mf
soul!
Glor-y! Glor-y!
Glor-y, oh my soul!
Glor-y! Glory!
18
mp
23
Don't you wan-na go where gates are pearl and streets are paved with gold where

26
God shall wipe all tears and death shall be no more Glor-y! Glor-y!
30
C
cantabile
Glor - y, oh my soul! Oh Glor - y!
35
Oh Glor-y! There is room e-nough in par-a-dise to

39
D
freely
have a home in Glor - y!
Mm
Mm
Pno.
44
Mm
Mm
I have a home in
Pno.
48
E Joyfully (♩ = 80)
mf
Glo ry!
I got a new name o - ver in
Pno.
mf

51
glor - y and it's mine, mine, all mine! I got a
51
54
new name o - ver in glor - y and it's mine, mine, all mine!
54
57
Oh I got a new home o - ver in glor - y and it's
57

F
mine, mine, all mine! I got a new home o - ver in
Pno.
Tempo Primo (♩ = 60)
glor - y where gates are pearl and streets are paved with gold, where
Pno.
God shall wipe all tears and death shall be no more!
Pno.

69
Glor-y! Glor-y! Don't you wan - na go?
69

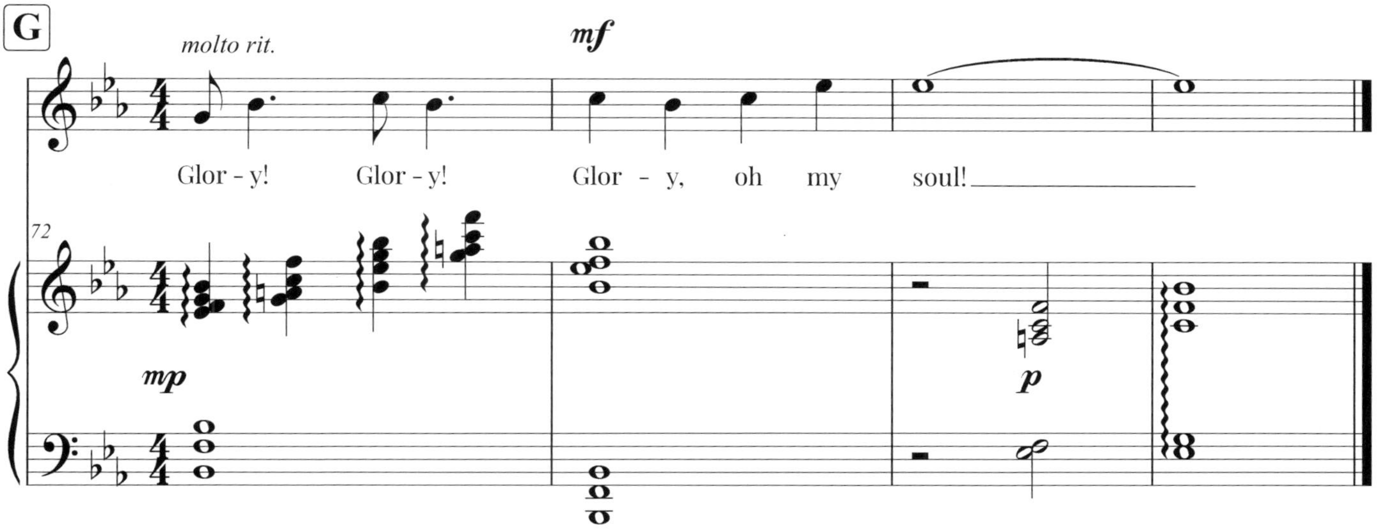
G
molto rit.
mf
Glor - y! Glor - y! Glor - y, oh my soul!
72
mp
p

City Called Heaven

for Medium Voice

Negro Spiritual
Arranged by Colin Lett

City Called Heaven

20
f
times I am toss - ed and driv-en, Lord, Some - times I don't know where to
Pno.
mf
23
dim.
mp
roam, I heard of a cit - y called Heav - en, I've
p
26
1.
f
start - ed to make it my home. Some -

City Called Heaven

Deep River

for Medium Voice

Negro Spiritual
Arranged by Colin Lett

15
2.
mf
Oh, don't you want to go to that Gos - pel
mp
19
rit.
feast, that Prom - ised Lan' where all is
rit.
23
l'istesso tempo
peace? Oh, Deep riv - er, Lord, I
l'istesso tempo

26
rit.
want to cross o - ver in - to camp - ground, Lord, I
Pno.
rit.
28
mp molto rit.
dolce
a tempo
want to cross o - ver in - to camp - ground.
Pno.
molto rit.
a tempo

Blank Page

Fix Me, Jesus

for Medium Voice

Negro Spiritual
Arranged by Colin Lett

Second Time To Coda
Fix me for my star - ry crown. Fix me, Je - sus, fix me.
Fix me for a high - er ground.
Second Time To Coda
mf
Oh, fix me; Oh, fix me;
mf
Oh, fix me, Lord; fix me, Je - sus, fix me.

27
mf
Fix me, Je-sus, fix me, Lord. Fix me, Je-sus, fix me, Lord.
Pno.
mf

31
Fix me, Je-sus, fix me, Lord. Fix me, Je-sus, fix me.
Pno.

35
mp rit.
Fix me, Je-sus, fix me. Fix me. Fix me, Je-sus.
Pno.

MM-022

Give Me Jesus

for Medium Voice

Negro Spiritual
Arranged by Colin Lett

mf
C
have all this world, give me Je - sus. Dark mid - night was my
Vln.
mf
Pno.
mf
cry, Dark mid-night was my cry, Dark mid-night was my cry, Give me Je -
Vln.
Pno.
p
D
con affetto
poco a poco cresc.
mf
sus. Give me Je - sus. Give me Je - sus. You may have all this
Vln.
p
mp
Pno.
p
poco a poco cresc.

E Freely, Broader
f
mf
world, give me Je - sus. Oh, when I come to die, Oh,
when I come to die, Oh, when I come to die, Give me Je -
F
sus. Give me Je - sus. Give me Je - sus. You may have all this

G
world, give me Je - - sus.
Vln.
Pno.
mf
mf
mp
mp

Violin

Give Me Jesus

for Medium Voice

Negro Spiritual

Arranged by Colin Lett

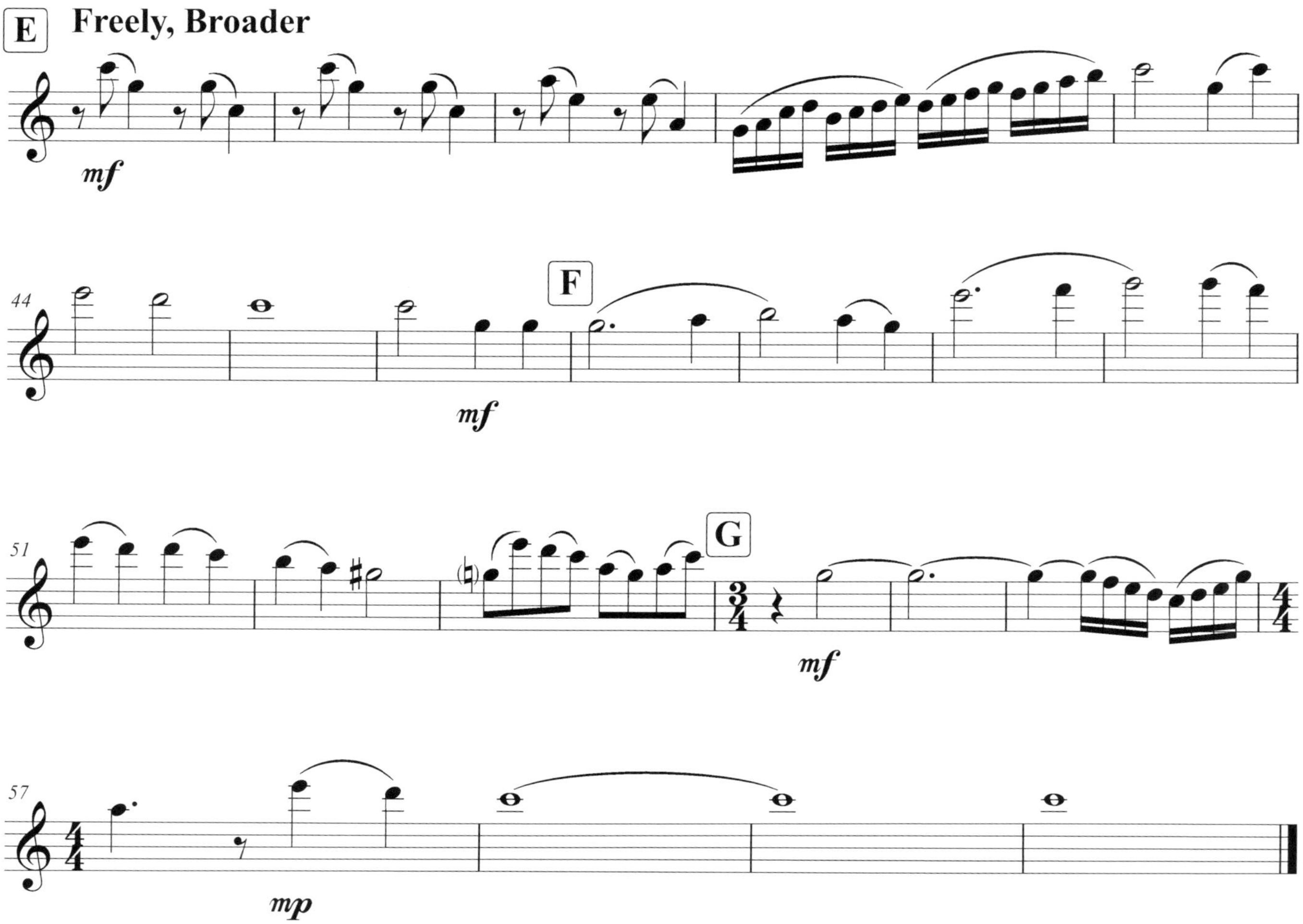
E
Freely, Broader
mf
44
F
mf
51
G
mf
57
mp

MM-022

I Got a Robe

for Medium Voice

Negro Spiritual
Arranged by Colin Lett

17
Heav-en, Heav-en, Ev' - ry-bo-dy talk-in' 'bout Heav'n ain' go-in' there,
Pno.
21
Heav-en, Heav-en, I'm gon-na shout all o - ver God's Heav-en.
walk
Pno.
25
1.
Pno.

28
2.
I got a crown, You got a crown, All
32
o' God's chil-lun got a crown. When I get to Heav-en gon-na put on my crown, I'm gon-na
36
shout all o - ver God's Heav-en, Heav-en, Heav-en, Ev' -

40
- ry-bo-dy talk-in' 'bout Heav'n ain' go-in' there, Heav-en, Heav-en, I'm gon-na
Pno.
44
shout all o - ver God's Heav-en.
f
I got a song, You
Pno.
48
got a song, All o' God's chil-lun got a song. When I get to Heav-en gon-na
Pno.

ad lib.
sing a new song, I'm gon-na sing all o-ver God's Heav-en, Heav-en, Oh, Ev' -
- ry-bo-dy talk-in' 'bout Heav'n ain' go-in' there, Heav-en, Heav-en, I'm gon-na
shout all o - ver, walk all o - ver, sing all o - ver God's Heav-en!

In Bright Mansions Above

for Medium Voice

Negro Spiritual
Arranged by Colin Lett

*yonder

16
man - sions a - bove, In bright man - sions a - bove, Lord, I
mp
20
wan' to live up yon - dah, In bright man - sions a - bove.
24

mf
con dolore
My mo - ther's gone to glo - ry, I wan' to go there
Pno.
mf
risoluto
teneramente
too, Lord, I wan' to live up yon - dah in man - sions a -
mp
mf
mp
bove. In bright man - sions a - bove, In bright man - sions a - bove, Lord, I

42
wan' to live up yon - dah, up yon - dah, up yon -
42
46
p
molto legato
rit. to end
dah, in bright man - - - sions a bove.
46
p rit. to end
pp

Oh Mother, Don't You Weep

for Medium Voice

Negro Spiritual
Arranged by Colin Lett

Oh Mother, Don't You Weep

32
teneramente
p
Oh mo-ther, don' you weep when I am gone. When I'm
Pno.
32
p
37
gone, When I'm gone, Oh mo - ther, don' you
Pno.
37
42
p
n
weep when I am gone, gone, when I'm gone.
Pno.
42
n
Ped.
*

MM-022

Swing Low, Sweet Chariot

for Medium Voice

Negro Spritual
Arranged by Colin Lett

Swing Low, Sweet Chariot

24
home, But still my soul feels Heav'n - ly bound, Come to car - ry me
24
ritenuto
28
rit.
freely
a tempo
home. Mm, Swing low, Sweet
28
a tempo
31
char - i - ot, Com - in' for to car - ry me home, Swing
31

34
low, Sweet char - i - ot, Com - in' for to car - ry me home. Mm,
34
Pno.

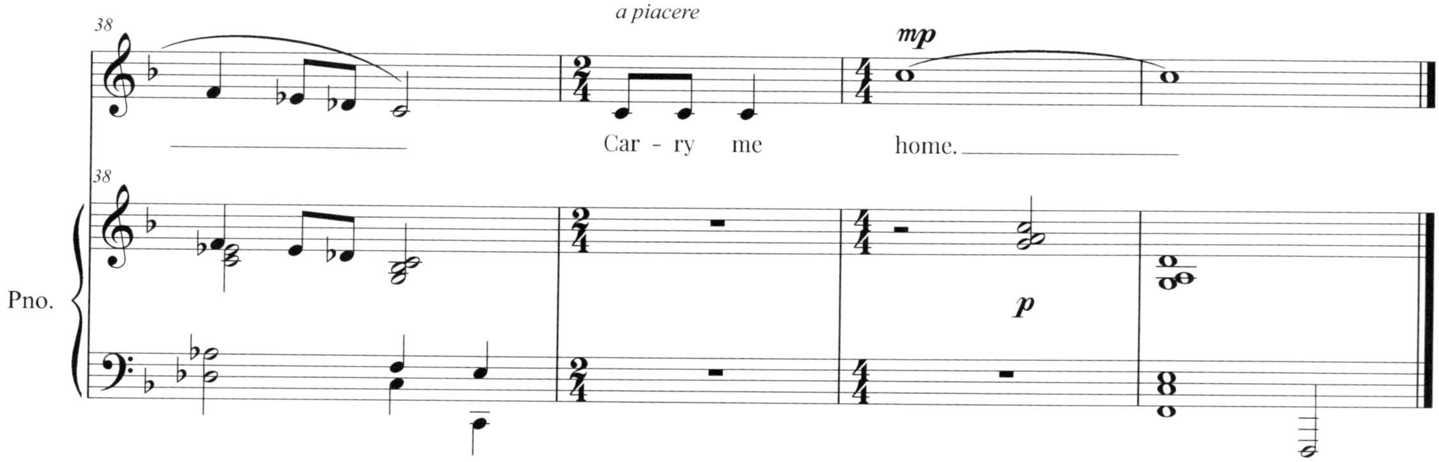
38
a piacere
mp
Car - ry me home.
38
Pno.
p

Tryin' to Get Home

for Medium Voice

Negro Spiritual
Arranged by Colin Lett

13
bear - in' heav-y bur - dens, Lord, I'm bear - in' heav-y bur - dens, Lord, I'm
13
Pno.
17
freely
mf
bear - in' heav-y bur - dens, Try'n t' get home. Lord, I'm
17
Pno.
with forward motion
mp
21
climb - in' high moun - tains, Try'n t' get home. Lord, I'm
21
Pno.

25
climb - in' high moun - tains, Try'n t' get home. Lord, I'm
29
climb - in' high moun - tains, Lord, I'm climb - in' high moun - tains, Lord, I'm
33
climb - in' high moun - tains, Try'n t' get home. Lord, I
poco rit.
poco rit.

affectuoso
wonder if I'll ever reach my home, reach my home. Lord, I
Pno.
a tempo
wonder if I'll ever reach my home, reach my home. Lord, I'm
mp
Pno.
rit. to end
bearin' heavy burdens, Try'n t' get home.
p
pp
Pno.
rit. to end
pp

Made in the USA
Columbia, SC
07 April 2025

56228238R00028